HOW TO HELP THE PLANET

STOPPING POLLUTION

by
Rebecca Phillips-Bartlett

BEARPORT
PUBLISHING

Minneapolis, Minnesota

Credits: All images are courtesy of Shutterstock.com, unless otherwise specified. With thanks to Getty Images, Thinkstock Photo, and iStockphoto. Recurring images – VectorMine, Anna Kosheleva, Maksym Drozd. Cover – VectorMine, Dmytro Zinkevych. 2–3 – Sunny studio. 4–5 – Tridsanu Thopet, vovidzha. 6–7 – Rich Carey, Maples Images. 8–9 – vchal, newphotoservice. 10–11 – focal point, jantsarik. 12–13 – Rawpixel.com, wavebreakmedia. 14–15 – Olga Miltsova, amenic181, MichaelJayBerlin, Valentina Proskurina, valzan, freeskyline, Tanya Sid, ElenaPhotos, Jerome.Romme, Daisy Daisy. 16–17 – debasige, Alrandir, Maria Symchych, Elena Chevalier, DyrElena, Troyan. 18–19 – Monkey Business Images, Stock-Asso. 20–21 – photka, wavebreakmedia. 22–23 – paulaphoto, Inside Creative House.

Bearport Publishing Company Product Development Team
President: Jen Jenson; Director of Product Development: Spencer Brinker; Managing Editor: Allison Juda; Associate Editor: Naomi Reich; Associate Editor: Tiana Tran; Senior Designer: Colin O'Dea; Designer: Elena Klinkner; Designer: Kayla Eggert; Product Development Assistant: Owen Hamlin

Library of Congress Cataloging-in-Publication Data is available at www.loc.gov or upon request from the publisher.

ISBN: 979-8-88916-287-2 (hardcover)
ISBN: 979-8-88916-292-6 (paperback)
ISBN: 979-8-88916-296-4 (ebook)

© 2024 BookLife Publishing
This edition is published by arrangement with BookLife Publishing.

North American adaptations © 2024 Bearport Publishing Company. All rights reserved. No part of this publication may be reproduced in whole or in part, stored in any retrieval system, or transmitted in any form or by any means, electronic, mechanical, photocopying, recording, or otherwise, without written permission from the publisher.

For more information, write to Bearport Publishing, 5357 Penn Avenue South, Minneapolis, MN 55419.

CONTENTS

Our Planet, Our Pollution 4
There Is Plenty We Can Do 6
How to Plan a Litter Pickup 8
What Happens to Our Waste? . . 10
Let's Compost 12
What Is Recycling? 14
How to Recycle 16
Know Your Plastic 18
How to Upcycle 20
We Can Help 22
Glossary 24
Index 24

OUR PLANET, OUR POLLUTION

Earth is our home. It gives us everything we need to live. The planet takes care of us, but we are not always good at taking care of it.

We have made the planet unhealthy with lots of **pollution**. These are things we make and leave around that make Earth dirty. What can we do to help fight pollution?

Trees help clean the air, but pollution stops young trees from growing.

THERE IS PLENTY WE CAN DO

Pollution can be on the ground, in the oceans, or in the air.

Pollution is a problem, but we can still work together to clean up the planet. Even the smallest things can make a difference.

There are plenty of ways to get rid of our waste and stop pollution. Let's learn about some of the best ways to make Earth healthier.

HOW TO PLAN A LITTER PICKUP

Litter is a very common kind of pollution. It is trash people leave where it does not belong. But you can help by planning a litter pickup!

Litter pickups help clean up the planet. Gather a group of friends and a grown-up. Together, clean up outside!

Litter pickers and gloves keep us safe as we pick up trash.

WHAT HAPPENS TO OUR WASTE?

We throw many things into the garbage. This trash ends up in **landfills**, where it is often buried under the ground.

A LANDFILL

Landfills harm the planet because they let out lots of **greenhouse gases**. These gases trap heat around Earth. This can make the planet warmer and speed up **climate change**.

Some landfills have wells that collect a greenhouse gas called methane.

LET'S COMPOST

Sometimes, we make or buy too much food. What we do not eat might go to landfills. But we can help! Let's turn our food waste into **compost** that can be used to grow new food.

Compost becomes healthy dirt.

There are many ways to make compost from food waste. We can do it in our backyard or drop off the waste at a local compost area. Get a grown-up to help decide which one works best for you!

THINGS YOU CAN COMPOST

Vegetable peels
Tea bags
Leaves
Fruit

THINGS YOU CANNOT COMPOST

Meat and fish
Cooked food
Dairy

WHAT IS RECYCLING?

Recycling is taking something old and making it into something new. Cans, bottles, and paper are collected at recycling centers.

Recycling makes less waste for landfills. This helps the planet by causing less pollution and greenhouse gases. Recycling also means we get as much use from everything as possible.

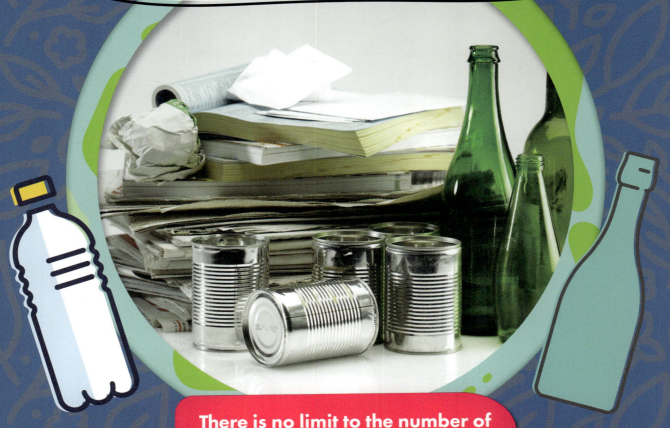

There is no limit to the number of times we can recycle metal cans.

HOW TO RECYCLE

Many things can be recycled, but there are some things we cannot recycle. Ask a grown-up what you can recycle where you live.

In most places, paper, cardboard, and cans are okay to recycle. Some places let people recycle even more! Make a poster to show what can be recycled where you live.

Things you want to recycle must be clean and dry.

KNOW YOUR PLASTIC

Single-use plastic things, such as forks and straws, can be used only once. They are often made of plastic we cannot recycle. These things stay in the environment for years.

Half of all plastic made is single-use!

Try replacing single-use plastic things with ones that can be reused. Use a metal straw instead of a plastic one.

How much plastic does your family use in a week?

HOW TO UPCYCLE

Another way to avoid problems of single-use plastic is to **upcycle**. This means taking something old and using it in a new way. When we upcycle, it helps save the planet and lets us get creative at the same time!

Plastic toys are made in factories that make a lot of greenhouse gases. Why not make your own toys? You can upcycle old plastic bottles, metal cans, or cardboard tubes into new toys.

Gather paint and other art supplies to decorate your new toys.

WE CAN HELP

Pollution is a big problem for our planet. However, there are plenty of things we can do to help. A lot of the waste that we throw away can be turned into something new.

Recycling, composting, and upcycling are just some of the things we can do to help the planet. The small things we do will make a big change!

What will you do to help the planet?

GLOSSARY

climate change the change to Earth's weather patterns

compost material made of rotted plants and food that can be used to make soil better

greenhouse gases gases that trap heat around Earth

landfills large holes in the ground used for dumping trash

litter trash that has been left on the ground

methane a gas that comes from rotting waste

pollution anything that makes Earth unhealthy or dirty

recycling turning something old into something new

single-use plastic plastic made to be used once and then thrown away

upcycle to make something used into something different

INDEX

air 5–6
Earth 4–5, 7, 11
environment 18
greenhouse gases 11, 15, 21
ground 6, 10
landfills 10–12, 15
litter 8–9
plastic 18–21
pollution 5–8, 15, 22
trash 8–10